The Very Best of Winston Churchill

Quotes from a British Legend

SIMON PAIGE

DEDICATION

This book is dedicated to Winston Churchill, a true legend of British history and an inspiration to many since.

CONTENTS

1 INTRODUCTION

Winston Churchill is a name known across the world and one of the most revered leaders in history. Naturally, he is probably best known for being such as instrumental part of the defence of Britain during World War II.

However, as well as being a great leader, Churchill was also known for his many well-publicised quotes, providing a thought-provoking, interesting and humorous look into the mind of this unique personality.

This book brings together some of the best of these quotes, from his opinions on war to his general philosophy on life.

Though these quotes are from a lifetime ago, many hold as true today as the day on which he said them. It's clear from his words that Churchill was as much of a philosopher as he was a politician.

All of the quotes within this book are words spoken by the man himself.

2 ABOUT HIMSELF

"I have nothing to offer but blood, toil, tears and sweat."

*

"My wife and I tried two or three times in the last 40 years to have breakfast together, but it was so disagreeable we had to stop."

*

"Ending a sentence with a preposition is something up with which I will not put."

*

"I am fond of pigs. Dogs look up to us. Cats look down on us. Pigs treat us as equals."

*

"We are all worms. But I believe that I am a glow-worm."

*

"Personally I'm always ready to learn, although I do not always like being taught."

*

"My most brilliant achievement was my ability to be able to persuade my wife to marry me."

*

"I was only the servant of my country and had I, at any moment, failed to express her unflinching resolve to fight and conquer, I should at once have been rightly cast aside."

*

4

"I am certainly not one of those who need to be prodded. In fact, if anything, I am the prod."

*

"History will be kind to me for I intend to write it."

*

"I am always ready to learn although I do not always like being taught."

*

"Although prepared for martyrdom, I preferred that it be postponed."

*

"I always seem to get inspiration and renewed vitality by contact with this great novel land of yours which sticks up out of the Atlantic."

*

"I am an optimist. It does not seem too much use being anything else."

*

"I never worry about action, but only inaction."

*

"I like a man who grins when he fights."

*

"In the course of my life, I have often had to eat my words, and I must confess that I have always found it a wholesome diet."

*

"I have been brought up and trained to have the utmost contempt for people who get drunk."

*

"I am easily satisfied with the very best."

*

"I am prepared to meet my Maker. Whether my Maker is prepared for the great ordeal of meeting me is another matter."

*

"Eating words has never given me indigestion."

*

"I always avoid prophesying beforehand, because it is a much better policy to prophesy after the event has already taken place."

*

"I cannot pretend to be impartial about the colours. I rejoice with the brilliant ones, and am genuinely sorry for the poor browns."

*

"Really I feel less keen about the Army every day. I think the Church would suit me better."

*

"I have taken more out of alcohol than alcohol has taken out of me."

3 ABOUT OTHER PEOPLE

"Baldwin thought Europe was a bore, and Chamberlain thought it was only a greater Birmingham."

*

"Meeting Franklin Roosevelt was like opening your first bottle of champagne; knowing him was like drinking it."

*

"My rule of life prescribed as an absolutely sacred rite smoking cigars and also the drinking of alcohol before, after and if need be during all meals and in the intervals between them."

*

"Mr. Attlee is a very modest man. Indeed he has a lot
to be modest about."

4 ABOUT POLITICS

"Politics are very much like war. We may even have to use poison gas at times."

*

"In war, you can only be killed once, but in politics, many times."

*

"Politics is almost as exciting as war, and quite as dangerous. In war you can only be killed once, but in politics many times."

*

"A politician needs the ability to foretell what is going to happen tomorrow, next week, next month, and next year. And to have the ability afterwards to explain why it didn't happen."

*

"The inherent vice of capitalism is the unequal sharing of blessings; the inherent virtue of socialism is the equal sharing of miseries."

*

"No part of the education of a politician is more indispensable than the fighting of elections."

*

"Politics is the ability to foretell what is going to happen tomorrow, next week, next month and next year. And to have the ability afterwards to explain why it didn't happen."

*

"It is a fine game to play - the game of politics - and it is well worth waiting for a good hand before really plunging."

*

"I am never going to have anything more to do with politics or politicians. When this war is over I shall confine myself entirely to writing and painting."

*

"Socialism is a philosophy of failure, the creed of ignorance, and the gospel of envy, its inherent virtue is the equal sharing of misery."

*

"Nothing can be more abhorrent to democracy than to imprison a person or keep him in prison because he is unpopular. This is really the test of civilization."

*

"Politics is not a game. It is an earnest business."

*

"It has been said that democracy is the worst form of government except all the others that have been tried."

5 GENERAL PHILOSOPHY

"Sure I am of this, that you have only to endure to conquer."

*

"No crime is so great as daring to excel."

*

"You have enemies? Good. That means you've stood up for something, sometime in your life."

*

"It was the nation and the race dwelling all round the globe that had the lion's heart. I had the luck to be called upon to give the roar."

*

"It is no use saying, 'We are doing our best.' You have got to succeed in doing what is necessary."

*

"Men occasionally stumble over the truth, but most of them pick themselves up and hurry off as if nothing had happened."

*

"The price of greatness is responsibility."

*

"To improve is to change; to be perfect is to change often."

*

"Some people regard private enterprise as a predatory tiger

to be shot. Others look on it as a cow they can milk. Not enough people see it as a healthy horse, pulling a sturdy wagon."

*

"Success consists of going from failure to failure without loss of enthusiasm."

*

"Solitary trees, if they grow at all, grow strong."

*

"Without tradition, art is a flock of sheep without a shepherd. Without innovation, it is a corpse."

*

"From Stettin in the Baltic to Trieste in the Adriatic, an iron curtain has descended across the Continent."

*

"History is written by the victors."

*

"Do not let spacious plans for a new world divert your energies from saving what is left of the old."

*

"If you're going through hell, keep going."

*

"India is a geographical term. It is no more a united nation than the Equator."

*

"This is no time for ease and comfort. It is time to dare and endure."

*

"An appeaser is one who feeds a crocodile, hoping it will eat him last."

*

"There is no such thing as a good tax."

*

"It is a mistake to look too far ahead. Only one link of the chain of destiny can be handled at a time."

*

"Now this is not the end. It is not even the beginning of the end. But it is, perhaps, the end of the beginning."

*

"Victory at all costs, victory in spite of all terror, victory however long and hard the road may be; for without victory, there is no survival."

*

"A man does what he must - in spite of personal consequences, in spite of obstacles and dangers and pressures - and that is the basis of all human morality."

*

"We have always found the Irish a bit odd. They refuse to be English."

*

"We shall draw from the heart of suffering itself the means of inspiration and survival."

*

"Short words are best and the old words when short are best of all."

*

"Too often the strong, silent man is silent only because he does not know what to say, and is reputed strong only because he has remained silent."

*

"A fanatic is one who can't change his mind and won't change the subject."

*

"The farther backward you can look, the farther forward

you can see."

*

"Man will occasionally stumble over the truth, but most of the time he will pick himself up and continue on."

*

"Russia is a riddle wrapped in a mystery inside an enigma."

*

"Healthy citizens are the greatest asset any country can have."

*

"If you have ten thousand regulations you destroy all respect for the law."

*

"It is more agreeable to have the power to give than to receive."

*

"We shall show mercy, but we shall not ask for it."

*

"Never, never, never give up."

*

"No idea is so outlandish that it should not be considered with a searching but at the same time a steady eye."

*

"We are asking the nations of Europe between whom rivers of blood have flowed to forget the feuds of a thousand years."

*

"What kind of people do they think we are? Is it possible they do not realize that we shall never cease to persevere against them until they have been taught a lesson which they and the world will never forget?"

*

"The truth is incontrovertible. Malice may attack it, ignorance may deride it, but in the end, there it is."

*

"We make a living by what we get, but we make a life by what we give."

*

"'No comment' is a splendid expression. I am using it again and again."

*

"Courage is rightly esteemed the first of human qualities... because it is the quality which guarantees all others."

*

"We shape our buildings; thereafter they shape us."

*

"We do not covet anything from any nation except their

respect."

*

"Difficulties mastered are opportunities won."

*

"Study history, study history. In history lies all the secrets of statecraft."

*

"If you have an important point to make, don't try to be subtle or clever. Use a pile driver. Hit the point once. Then come back and hit it again. Then hit it a third time - a tremendous whack."

*

"Continuous effort - not strength or intelligence - is the key to unlocking our potential."

*

"These are not dark days: these are great days - the greatest days our country has ever lived."

*

"Attitude is a little thing that makes a big difference."

*

"There is no such thing as public opinion. There is only published opinion."

*

"Courage is what it takes to stand up and speak; courage is also what it takes to sit down and listen."

*

"We are masters of the unsaid words, but slaves of those we let slip out."

*

"One ought never to turn one's back on a threatened danger and try to run away from it. If you do that, you will double the danger. But if you meet it promptly and without flinching, you will reduce the danger by half. Never run away from anything. Never!"

*

"The empires of the future are the empires of the mind."

*

"However beautiful the strategy, you should occasionally look at the results."

*

"The first quality that is needed is audacity."

*

"It is a fine thing to be honest, but it is also very important to be right."

*

"To build may have to be the slow and laborious task of years. To destroy can be the thoughtless act of a single day."

*

"A joke is a very serious thing."

*

"The power of man has grown in every sphere, except over himself."

*

"We are stripped bare by the curse of plenty."

*

"Perhaps it is better to be irresponsible and right, than to be responsible and wrong."

*

"Success is not final, failure is not fatal: it is the courage to continue that counts."

*

"For my part, I consider that it will be found much better by all parties to leave the past to history, especially as I propose to write that history myself."

*

"All the great things are simple, and many can be expressed in a single word: freedom, justice, honor, duty, mercy, hope."

*

"It is always wise to look ahead, but difficult to look further than you can see."

*

"Everyone has his day and some days last longer than others."

*

"One does not leave a convivial party before closing time."

*

"Great and good are seldom the same man."

*

"A lie gets halfway around the world before the truth has a chance to get its pants on."

*

"Although personally I am quite content with existing explosives, I feel we must not stand in the path of improvement."

*

"The short words are best, and the old words are the best of all."

*

"If the Almighty were to rebuild the world and asked me for advice, I would have English Channels round every country. And the atmosphere would be such that anything which attempted to fly would be set on fire."

*

"Let our advance worrying become advance thinking and planning."

*

"Criticism may not be agreeable, but it is necessary. It fulfils the same function as pain in the human body. It calls attention to an unhealthy state of things."

*

"The British nation is unique in this respect. They are the only people who like to be told how bad things are, who like to be told the worst."

*

"It is a good thing for an uneducated man to read books of quotations."

*

"Kites rise highest against the wind - not with it."

*

"Broadly speaking, the short words are the best, and the old words best of all."

*

"The reserve of modern assertions is sometimes pushed to extremes, in which the fear of being contradicted leads the writer to strip himself of almost all sense and meaning."

*

"A pessimist sees the difficulty in every opportunity; an optimist sees the opportunity in every difficulty."

*

"If we open a quarrel between past and present, we shall find that we have lost the future."

*

"The pessimist sees difficulty in every opportunity. The optimist sees the opportunity in every difficulty."

*

"True genius resides in the capacity for evaluation of uncertain, hazardous, and conflicting information."

*

"If the human race wishes to have a prolonged and indefinite period of material prosperity, they have only got to behave in a peaceful and helpful way toward one another."

*

"Never hold discussions with the monkey when the organ grinder is in the room."

*

"Play the game for more than you can afford to lose... only then will you learn the game."

6 HUMOROUS

"There are two things that are more difficult than making an after-dinner speech: climbing a wall which is leaning toward you and kissing a girl who is leaning away from you."

*

"The best argument against democracy is a five-minute conversation with the average voter."

*

"If Hitler invaded hell I would make at least a favourable reference to the devil in the House of Commons."

*

"When I am abroad, I always make it a rule never to criticize or attack the government of my own country. I make up for lost time when I come home."

*

"You can always count on Americans to do the right thing - after they've tried everything else."

*

"There are a terrible lot of lies going about the world, and the worst of it is that half of them are true."

*

"The length of this document defends it well against the risk of its being read."

*

"I'm just preparing my impromptu remarks."

*

"I may be drunk, Miss, but in the morning I will be sober and you will still be ugly."

7 ON WAR

"Never in the field of human conflict was so much owed by so many to so few."

*

"Battles are won by slaughter and maneuver. The greater the general, the more he contributes in maneuver, the less he demands in slaughter."

*

"Nothing in life is so exhilarating as to be shot at without result."

*

"A prisoner of war is a man who tries to kill you and fails, and then asks you not to kill him."

*

"War is mainly a catalogue of blunders."

*

"We shall defend our island, whatever the cost may be, we shall fight on the beaches, we shall fight on the landing grounds, we shall fight in the fields and in the streets, we shall fight in the hills; we shall never surrender."

*

"When you have to kill a man, it costs nothing to be polite."

*

"In wartime, truth is so precious that she should always be attended by a bodyguard of lies."

*

"The power of an air force is terrific when there is nothing to oppose it."

*

"In war as in life, it is often necessary when some cherished scheme has failed, to take up the best alternative open, and if so, it is folly not to work for it with all your might."

*

"The great defense against the air menace is to attack the enemy's aircraft as near as possible to their point of departure."

*

"War is a game that is played with a smile. If you can't smile, grin. If you can't grin, keep out of the way till you can."

*

"When you are winning a war almost everything that happens can be claimed to be right and wise."

*

"When the war of the giants is over the wars of the pygmies will begin."

*

"The problems of victory are more agreeable than those of defeat, but they are no less difficult."

*

"Those who can win a war well can rarely make a good peace and those who could make a good peace would never have won the war."

*

"Before Alamein we never had a victory. After Alamein we never had a defeat."

*

"To jaw-jaw is always better than to war-war."

*

"If you go on with this nuclear arms race, all you are going to do is make the rubble bounce."

*

"For good or for ill, air mastery is today the supreme expression of military power and fleets and armies, however vital and important, must accept a subordinate rank."

ABOUT THE AUTHOR

Simon Paige is a very silly man who writes very silly books and very silly articles on the internet. He is also a fond admirer of history as well as very silly comedy.

Made in the USA
Las Vegas, NV
15 August 2021